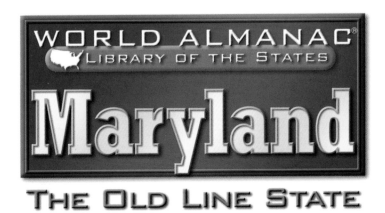

THE OLD LINE STATE

by Michael A. Martin

Curriculum Consultant: Jean Craven,
Director of Instructional Support,
Albuquerque, NM, Public Schools

WORLD ALMANAC® LIBRARY

Please visit our web site at: **www.worldalmanaclibrary.com**
For a free color catalog describing World Almanac® Library's
list of high-quality books and multimedia programs, call
1-800-848-2928 (USA) or 1-800-387-3178 (Canada).
World Almanac® Library's fax: (414) 332-3567.

Library of Congress Cataloging-in-Publication Data

Martin, Michael A.
    Maryland, the Old Line State / by Michael A. Martin.
      p. cm. — (World Almanac Library of the states)
    Includes bibliographical references and index.
    Summary: Illustrations and text present the history, geography, people, politics and
government, economy, and social life and customs of Maryland.
    ISBN 0-8368-5137-4 (lib. bdg.)
    ISBN 0-8368-5307-5 (softcover)
    1. Maryland—Juvenile literature. [1. Maryland.] I. Title. II. Series.
F181.3.M37   2002
975.2—dc21   2002023453

This edition first published in 2002 by
World Almanac® Library
330 West Olive Street, Suite 100
Milwaukee, WI 53212 USA

Design and Editorial: Bill SMITH STUDIO Inc.
Editor: Timothy Paulson
Assistant Editor: Megan Elias
Art Director: Jay Jaffe
Photo Research: Sean Livingstone
World Almanac® Library Project Editor: Patricia Lantier
World Almanac® Library Editors: Monica Rausch, Lymon Lyons, Catherine Gardner
World Almanac® Library Production: Scott M. Krall, Tammy Gruenewald,
  Katherine A. Goedheer

Printed in the United States of America

1 2 3 4 5 6 7 8 9 06 05 04 03 02

Maryland

INTRODUCTION	4
ALMANAC	6
HISTORY	8
THE PEOPLE	16
THE LAND	20
ECONOMY & COMMERCE	24
POLITICS & GOVERNMENT	28
CULTURE & LIFESTYLE	32
NOTABLE PEOPLE	38
TIME LINE	42
STATE EVENTS & ATTRACTIONS	44
MORE ABOUT MARYLAND	46
INDEX	47

A Model for the Nation

Since its founding in 1634, Maryland has played a central role in U.S. history. During the Revolutionary War, General George Washington praised Maryland's "troops of the line," saluting them for their courage and determination. Maryland took its nickname — the Old Line State — from Washington's praise and committed itself to being actively involved in national affairs. In this spirit, Maryland provided the United States with two of its temporary national capitals — Baltimore and Annapolis — and donated the land on which the permanent capital, Washington, D.C., was built.

It was while watching a British attack on Baltimore during the War of 1812 that Francis Scott Key wrote "The Star-Spangled Banner," which would become the U.S. national anthem. As the nation matured and slavery became a central political and moral issue, the Mason–Dixon Line that divided Maryland from Pennsylvania became the symbol of all the differences between the North and South.

Maryland continues to play an important role in national and international politics. Students at the U.S. Naval Academy in Annapolis train to defend their country, while world leaders meet at Camp David to secure international peace.

Maryland has produced many world-renowned leaders, artists, and athletes, such as abolitionist Harriet Tubman, novelist Upton Sinclair, and baseball legend Cal Ripken, Jr. The picturesque state on the Chesapeake Bay, the home of old-fashioned crab boils, is also a modern powerhouse of industry and ideas. From the NASA Space Flight Center in Goddard to the American Visionary Art Museum in Baltimore, Maryland moves forward but always stays central to the nation's progress.

▶ Map of Maryland showing the interstate highway system, as well as major cities and waterways.

▼ Antietam National Battlefield was the site of a Civil War battle in 1862.

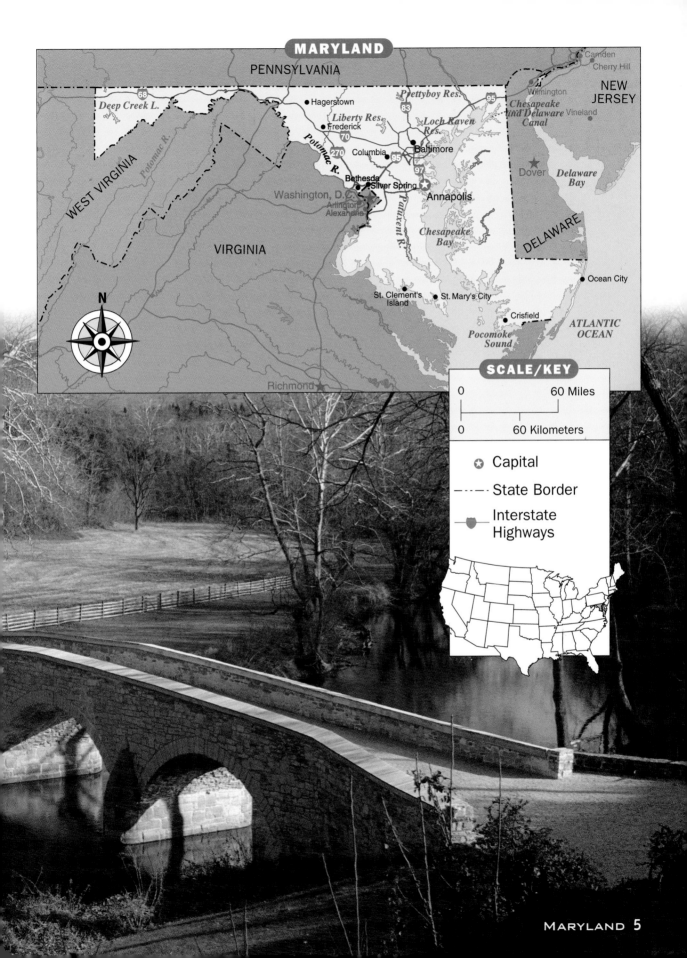

MARYLAND

PENNSYLVANIA

NEW JERSEY

Camden
Cherry Hill

Wilmington

Deep Creek L.

Hagerstown

Prettyboy Res.

68

83

95

Chesapeake and Delaware Canal

Vineland

WEST VIRGINIA

Potomac R.

Frederick

Liberty Res.

70

Loch Raven Res.

Baltimore

Columbia

95

Dover

Delaware Bay

270

7

97

Bethesda

Silver Spring

Annapolis

Washington, D.C.

Arlington
Alexandria

Patuxent R.

DELAWARE

VIRGINIA

Chesapeake Bay

Ocean City

N

St. Clement's Island

St. Mary's City

Crisfield

ATLANTIC OCEAN

Pocomoke Sound

Richmond

Fast Facts

MARYLAND (MD), The Old Line State

Entered Union

April 28, 1788 (7th state)

Capital	Population
Annapolis	35,838

Total Population (2000)

5,296,486 (19th most populous state) — *Between 1990 and 2000 the population of Maryland increased by 10.8 percent.*

Largest Cities	Population
Baltimore	651,154
Columbia	88,254
Silver Spring	76,540
Dundalk	62,306

Land Area

9,774 square miles (25,315 square kilometers) (42nd largest state)

State Motto

"Fatti Maschii, Parole Femine" — *Italian for* "Manly Deeds, Womanly Words" (*or* "Manly Deeds, Gentle Words").

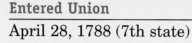

State Song

"Maryland, My Maryland," *by James Ryder Randall, adopted in 1939.*

State Bird

Baltimore oriole — *The male oriole's black and golden-orange plumage resembled the colors of Lord Baltimore's family shield, so the bird was called the Baltimore oriole.*

State Fish

Rockfish — *Also known as striped bass, this fish is of key importance to Maryland's fishing industry.*

State Insect

Baltimore checkerspot butterfly

State Tree

White oak

State Flower

Black-eyed Susan

State Dog

Chesapeake Bay retriever — *This breed of dog is one of the few to be developed in the United States. Strong and intelligent, it is used by hunters to recover waterfowl.*

State Cat

Calico cat — *The calico's orange, black, and white colors resemble both the coloring of the state bird and that of the state insect.*

State Crustacean

Maryland blue crab — *This crab thrives in the Chesapeake Bay's slightly salty waters and is integral to the state's economy.*

State Boat

Skipjack — *A sailing vessel with a single mast, used to harvest oysters.*

PLACES TO VISIT

NASA/Goddard Space Flight Center, Visitor Center and Museum, *Greenbelt*
See the rockets, space capsules, and artificial satellites of the U.S. space program close-up in this comprehensive space museum. Visitors are sometimes treated to launches of model rockets.

Chesapeake Bay Maritime Museum, *St. Michaels*
This attraction features a fully restored 1879 lighthouse, a saltwater aquarium, a waterfowl exhibit, and a collection of historic Chesapeake Bay boats and ships.

Inner Harbor Area, *Baltimore*
Attractions include the Maryland Science Center (which contains a museum and a planetarium), the National Aquarium, and a complex of shops and restaurants. The Harbor Area is also home to the USS *Constellation*, the only Civil War-era vessel still afloat.

For other places and events, see p. 44.

BIGGEST, BEST, AND MOST

- The Chesapeake Bay is North America's largest — and the world's second-largest — estuary.
- Opened for business in 1780, Maryland's State House is the nation's oldest continuously occupied state legislative building.

STATE FIRSTS

- **1784** Baltimore's Edward Warren took the first hot-air balloon trip in U.S. history. He was thirteen years old at the time.
- **1828** The nation's first umbrella factory opened in Baltimore. "Born in Baltimore, raised everywhere" became this new venture's slogan.
- **1851** In Baltimore, Jacob Fussell introduced packaged ice cream to the United States.

1812 Tall Tale

During the War of 1812, the town of St. Michaels supposedly pulled off an amazing trick. Knowing that the British were going to shell their town with cannon fire, the townsfolk hung lanterns high in treetops and blacked out all the lights in their houses. The British, mistaking the lantern lights for the lights of the town's buildings, aimed too high, and all but one of their cannonballs missed. The legend goes on to say that this was the first blackout in military history. More recent research, however, suggests that the legend is nothing more than a myth, and that the story was invented about the time of the battle's centennial. The residents of St. Michaels now acknowledge that instead of being the town that fooled the British, they're the town that fooled the tourists!

The Governor's Cup Crab Race

Every Labor Day weekend, crabs compete in derby-style races at the Governor's Cup Crab Race in Crisfield, "the Crab Capital of the World." In the main event, the National Hard Crab Derby, fifty-one crabs have their shells painted to represent each of the fifty states, plus Washington, D.C. Most of the crabs are blue crabs from Maryland's waters, but crabs from as far away as Hawaii have been flown in to take part. The governor's office presents a trophy to the winner.

America in Miniature

> Our fires are wood, our houses are good;
> Our diet is sawney and Homine.
> Drink, juice of the apple,
> tobacco's our staple.
> Gloria tibi Domine.
>
> — *Anonymous Marylander, pre-1740*

Native peoples first inhabited what would become Maryland more than ten thousand years ago. Although most Native Americans left as Europeans began to settle in the area, their names are still attached to many of Maryland's counties, towns, and rivers. During most of the first century of the colony's existence, relations with Native Americans were good, unlike the relations experienced in other settlements. In Jamestown, Virginia, for example, the early settlers fought with Native Americans.

European Exploration

Giovanni da Verrazano may have been the first European to see the Chesapeake Bay in 1524. Spanish Florida's governor, Pedro Menéndez de Avilés, is believed to have been the first to have explored it, in 1572. Captain John Smith, one of the founders of Jamestown, Virginia, followed in his footsteps in 1608 and wrote a detailed account of his travels in the region. William Claiborne, another Virginian, came to Chesapeake Bay's Kent Island in 1631 and opened a trading post, which became Maryland's first permanent European settlement. Kent Island was later disputed territory between the Maryland government and Virginia settlers.

Much of the next phase of Maryland's history was closely associated with the Calvert family of Yorkshire, England. In 1632, King Charles I of England granted a charter to George Calvert, the first Lord Baltimore, who was one of his most trusted advisers. This charter gave Calvert control of Maryland. Calvert died before the king

Native Americans of Maryland

Eastern Shore

Assateague

Choptank

Nanticoke

Pocomoke

Western Shore

Mattowoman

Piscataway

Potopaco

Taocomaco

Yaocomaco

Other Native American groups

Algonquin

Patuxent

Portobago

Susquehannock

Wicomico

could seal the charter, however, so Charles I gave the land to Calvert's son Cecilius, the second Lord Baltimore. Cecilius Calvert, the colony's proprietor, made his younger brother Leonard the colony's governor.

In March 1634, two Calvert ships, the *Ark* and the *Dove*, made landfall at St. Clement's Island in the Potomac River. Leonard Calvert bought land from the Yaocomaco, and the settlers — some 250 Roman Catholics and Protestants — founded what became St. Mary's City at the southern end of Maryland's western shore. St. Mary's served as Maryland's first capital until 1695, when Annapolis was made the capital.

The Struggle for Power

Maryland's early years were turbulent, in large part because of conflicts in England. In the 1640s, England was experiencing a civil war in which the king and his supporters, mainly Anglican and Roman Catholic, were opposed by forces, largely Puritan, who favored a stronger Parliament. The unrest in Maryland mirrored this tension.

The Calvert family was Roman Catholic, and although Leonard Calvert believed in religious freedom, many Maryland Protestants had trouble accepting Roman

▲ This painting of Baltimore Harbor in the 1800s shows both the region's beauty and the commercial importance of the harbor.

Catholic leadership. Challenges to the Calverts' authority were raised on religious grounds. In addition, neighboring colonies, such as Virginia, disputed Maryland's borders, complicating matters further.

As part of an attempt at reconciling Catholics and Protestants in Maryland, the colony passed what is known as the Act of Religious Toleration in 1649. The new law was written to make expressions of religious intolerance a crime. This legal support for religious freedom was one of the first documents of its kind in the colonies.

In 1654, a man named William Claiborne, who believed he had a stronger claim to Kent Island than the Calverts did, began a revolt that ousted them from power. Four years later, however, as the civil war was ending in England, that nation's new government forced Claiborne to hand power back. A revolt in 1689 led by John Coode and his Protestant Association eventually caused Charles Calvert, the third Lord of Baltimore, to lose control of the colony to the crown in 1691. In 1715, the crown gave control back to the Calvert family. The next Calvert was Protestant and less tolerant than Cecilius. The Calvert regime stripped Maryland's Roman Catholics of their voting rights in 1718, forbade them to hold office or worship publicly, and taxed them heavily. Catholics' rights would not be entirely restored until 1776, when Maryland's first constitution was written.

Drawing the Lines

In 1763, Maryland and the colony of Pennsylvania agreed to let a neutral party settle a dispute over their shared border. Charles Mason and Jeremiah Dixon, both Englishmen, surveyed the land and mapped the boundary, finishing their work in 1767. The border between the two colonies was dubbed the Mason and Dixon Line (later the Mason-Dixon Line) and has since served as the unofficial division between the northern and southern states.

Crowning Achievement

In the 1760s, Maryland and Pennsylvania hired Charles Mason and Jeremiah Dixon to survey their border. The men marked every fifth mile of the 233-mile (375-km) border between Maryland and Pennsylvania with a "crown stone," as shown below. The north face of each stone bore the Penn family shield and the south face, the Calvert family shield. Each mile in between was marked by a stone bearing a "P" on the north face and an "M" on the south face.

When the Mason-Dixon Line was resurveyed in the 1800s, it was found that the two men had done a remarkable job. Their original survey had taken five years and had been interrupted by battles with Native Americans, but the line never wavered more than 1.5 inches (3.8 cm) off the correct measurement.

Cry Revolution!

By the mid-1700s, the British government was deeply in debt. It tried to raise money by imposing new taxes and trade restrictions on its North American colonies. Like other colonists, Marylanders opposed these measures. For example, in 1773, they responded to the Boston Tea Act, which placed a tax on tea, by burning the tea-filled cargo ship *Peggy Stewart* while it was anchored at Annapolis.

Maryland sent delegates to the First Continental Congress in Philadelphia (1774) and supported a policy of interrupting British trade with the colonies. In May 1775 — just weeks after the battles at Lexington and Concord in Massachusetts — the Second Continental Congress assembled in Philadelphia. The Maryland delegates to this historic gathering voted for colonial independence on July 2, 1776. On November 8 of that same year, Maryland adopted its first constitution and elected its first governor, Thomas Johnson.

In December 1776, the British threatened to attack Philadelphia, and the Continental Congress moved to Baltimore, where it remained until March 1777. Throughout the Revolutionary War, Maryland soldiers fought bravely, and laborers in Baltimore worked to produce cannons and ships for the Continental armies.

As the Revolutionary War unfolded, the Continental Congress drafted the Articles of Confederation, the basis for the first U.S. government. Maryland delegates signed the document on March 1, 1781. John Hanson of Frederick served as the first president under the Articles and, from November 1783 to June 1784, Annapolis served as the capitol. In 1787, delegates from every state met in Philadelphia and drafted the U.S. Constitution, which Maryland ratified on April 28, 1788. It became the seventh state to enter the Union.

Charles Carroll

Charles Carroll (1737–1832) was born into a wealthy Catholic family in Annapolis. In 1774, he was elected to participate in the first Provincial Convention. Carroll became the first Roman Catholic to hold a government position in Maryland in more than one hundred years. The Convention chose Maryland's representatives to the First Continental Congress.

Even as late as 1776, not all Maryland landowners were ready to declare themselves free of British rule. Carroll, however, was a staunch advocate of independence. He convinced his fellow Marylanders to "[declare] the United States free and independent states."

That same year Carroll helped to write the Maryland constitution and later represented Maryland in the Continental Congress. He signed the Declaration of Independence on August 2, stating that he was willing "to defend the liberties of my country, or die with them."

From 1788 to 1791, he served as one of Maryland's U.S. senators. He was also a member of the Maryland Senate for many years. Carroll spent the last thirty years of his life as a businessman. When he died at age ninety-five, he had outlived every other person who had signed the Declaration of Independence.

The Rocket's Red Glare

Although the British never fought in Maryland during the Revolution, the state was the site of several crucial battles during the War of 1812. In 1813, British forces raided Maryland towns and farms along the Chesapeake. Maryland troops fought back bravely — although not always successfully.

In 1814, British General Robert Ross led a large contingent up the Patuxent River, defeating U.S. and Maryland forces on August 24 at the Battle of Bladensburg. Later that day, the British marched into Washington, D.C., where they burned the Capitol and the White House. In September, they attacked Baltimore. This time federal and Maryland forces prevailed, defending Baltimore and chasing the British out of the city. Francis Scott Key — a lawyer and poet born in Frederick, whose ship had been detained by the British navy — watched the battle unfold as he wrote "The Star-Spangled Banner."

Industry and Progress

Following the war Baltimore became an increasingly important transportation and industrial center, surpassing Annapolis in both population and commerce. Fast-sailing clipper ships were produced here early in the nineteenth century. Later the Baltimore and Ohio (B&O) Railroad moved goods from Baltimore to points west, while

Oh, Say Can You See

Fort McHenry was intended to serve as a point of defense for the city of Baltimore during the Revolutionary War. Baltimore was untouched by that war, but years later, Fort McHenry became famous as the site that inspired the U.S. national anthem. As Francis Scott Key watched the bombardment of the fort during the War of 1812, he was inspired to pen the poem that soon was set to music. It became the national anthem in 1931.

Today, Fort McHenry is the United States's only National Monument and Historic Shrine. The U.S. flag has flown there twenty-four hours a day, every day, since July 3, 1948.

eastbound products made their way from Baltimore on the Chesapeake and Delaware Canal. The *Tom Thumb*, the nation's first coal-burning steam locomotive, entered service in 1830 on the B&O Railroad's run from Baltimore to Ellicott's Mills (now Ellicott City). In 1839, the first U.S. oceangoing iron steamship was launched from Baltimore.

The Civil War and Slavery

Most states south of the Mason-Dixon Line began to secede from the Union in 1861, but Maryland did not. Many Marylanders, however, were sympathetic to the Confederate cause and joined the Confederacy's military forces. The state also did not outlaw slavery, which was illegal in the rest of the Union, until 1864.

Maryland was of great strategic importance to the Union. After Virginia's secession, Maryland was the only Union state between the newly formed Confederate States of America and the Union capital of Washington, D.C. Had Maryland joined the Confederacy, Washington would have been surrounded by foes.

Maryland was the site of several important Civil War battles. When General Robert E. Lee and his Confederate troops invaded Maryland in 1862, Union forces opposed them near Sharpsburg on September 17 at the Battle of Antietam. More than twelve thousand Union soldiers and some ten thousand Confederates died or were wounded — the bloodiest single day in the war's history.

The following day Lee withdrew his men to Virginia, but he crossed back into Maryland in June 1863 on his way to Gettysburg, Pennsylvania, where the Union Army handed him a decisive defeat. Confederate General Jubal A. Early and his troops entered Maryland after crossing the Potomac River in 1864; on July 9, Early's forces defeated a Union division near Frederick at the Battle of Monocacy. Early's men came within sight of Washington, D.C., before the Union Army rallied and pushed them back.

Following the Civil War, Maryland continued in its development as a key industrial and commercial center. Baltimore, already famous for its industrial prowess, gained fame for its contributions to the arts and

▶ An 1882 advertisement and timetable for the B&O Railroad.

culture during the latter half of the nineteenth century. Philanthropists such as financier Johns Hopkins, banker George Peabody, and iron merchant Enoch Pratt funded important cultural institutions: Johns Hopkins University, the Peabody Institute (later the Peabody Conservatory of Music), and the Enoch Pratt Free Library.

The Twentieth Century

Maryland's manufacturing and shipbuilding enterprises experienced boom times after the United States entered World War I in 1917. In that year the U.S. Army established its first testing center, the Aberdeen Proving Ground, along the Chesapeake Bay's northwest shore.

After the war the United States entered a period that became known as Prohibition. In 1919, the Eighteenth Amendment went into effect, prohibiting the manufacture, sale, and transportation of alcoholic beverages. Marylanders, however, rejected the amendment on the grounds that it violated the state's right to self-government. As a result, Maryland acquired another of its enduring nicknames: "the Free State." (Prohibition laws were finally repealed in 1933.)

The economic upheavals caused by the stock market collapse of 1929 devastated Maryland, crippling its industries. Thousands were out of work. The federal government responded by enacting social and economic

▼ Tanks were tested at the Aberdeen Proving Ground (APG) during the 1950s. APG, originally designed to test munitions for World War I, is the oldest proving ground in the nation.

▶ Baltimore's Inner Harbor was revitalized in the 1970s.

programs to get the country back on its feet. In 1937, families started moving into a new town called Greenbelt. The federal government sponsored the building of the town both to provide jobs and to provide housing for moderate-income families.

The U.S. entry into World War II in 1941 began to turn things around for Maryland's economy. Workers from neighboring states poured in to help fill the thousands of manufacturing jobs created by the urgent need for ships, armaments, and other goods. After the war's end in 1945, Maryland's population continued to grow, as did the state's prosperity. To accommodate so many new residents, Maryland concentrated on improving its cities and transportation systems.

In 1968, the city of Baltimore faced a crisis. Sparked by the assassination of Martin Luther King, Jr., riots broke out in the city and in other cities across the country. Baltimore had a difficult time recovering from the riots' aftermath, and the state as a whole faced hard times as major industrial and manufacturing businesses left the state. The 1970s were a time of economic depression for Maryland. One bright spot on the horizon was the redevelopment of the Baltimore waterfront. The Inner Harbor today is a famous tourist attraction and a source of great revenue.

New cities, suburbs, and industrial centers also sprang up between Baltimore and Washington, D.C. Maryland raced to provide these new areas with adequate services, including schools, water, and power. To raise money for these purposes, Maryland's voters approved a state lottery in 1972. Increasing pollution along the shores of the Chesapeake forced state officials to concentrate more than ever before on cleaning up the state's air and water — to help ensure that the Old Line State's best days were yet to come.

Capital Ties

Maryland's relationship with Washington, D.C., dates back to 1791, when Maryland donated land along the Potomac River to be used for the nation's capital. With improved transportation in the late nineteenth and early twentieth centuries, suburban communities grew up in the Maryland counties bordering Washington. Today, almost 90 percent of the state's population live in the combined D.C. suburban areas and the greater Baltimore metropolitan area. Marylanders commute into Washington to work in federal government jobs, and many federal agencies and offices, such as the Social Security Administration and the U.S. Census Bureau, are now located in the state.

Equality for All

> . . . an idea of equality also seems generally to prevail [in Maryland] and the inferior order of people pay but little external respect to those who occupy superior stations.
>
> — *William Eddis, an Englishman who landed in Maryland in 1769*

More than five million people live in Maryland — 5,296,486, to be exact, according to the 2000 U.S. Census. This places Maryland nineteenth among the states in terms of population, but the number of people in the state is growing more slowly than the national average. From 1990 to 2000, the population increased by 515,018, which works out to a growth rate of 10.8 percent, somewhat lower than the national average of 13.1 percent.

Maryland's Newcomers

During colonial times, the profitable tobacco-growing business drew new Maryland residents from many of the southern states. Prior to the Civil War, more free African Americans lived in Maryland than in any other state in the Union. The industrialization that characterized Baltimore

Age Distribution in Maryland (2000 Census)	
0–4	353,393
5–19	1,139,572
20–24	314,129
25–44	1,664,677
45–64	1,225,408
65 & over	599,307

Across One Hundred Years

Maryland's three largest foreign-born groups for 1890 and 1990

	1890	1990

Germany 52,436	Ireland 18,735	England 5,590	Korea 21,111	India 17,951	El Salvador 15,492

Total state population: 1,042,390
Total foreign-born: 94,296 (9%)

Total state population: 4,781,468
Total foreign-born: 313,494 (7%)

Patterns of Immigration

The total number of people who immigrated to Maryland in 1998 was 15,561. Of that number, the largest immigrant groups were from El Salvador (7.9%), India (7.1%), and Nigeria (6.4%).

from the 1830s forward drew thousands of workers from such European countries as Germany, Poland, Russia, England, and Ireland. Baltimore's Locust Point was second only to New York's Ellis Island as a point of entry for overseas immigrants. Throughout the nineteenth century, Maryland's population increased rapidly.

Maryland's population also grew during and after the World War II years. Population growth brought sweeping changes to the state, affecting everything from housing to education. During the mid-twentieth century, thousands of those who came to Maryland from southern states were African American.

A People Rich in Variety

More than one-quarter of Maryland's modern-day population is African American, over twice the national average. The majority of the remainder (64 percent) are

▲ Maryland's tobacco-growing industry attracted settlers in colonial times. As late as 1927, Maryland farm laborers used the same methods to cultivate and harvest tobacco that were used in colonial days.

Heritage and Background, Maryland — Year 2000

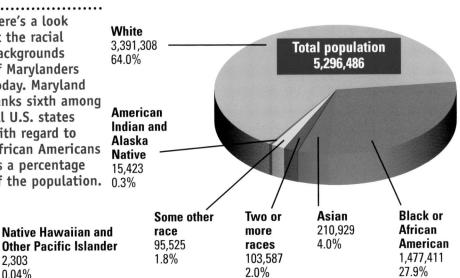

► Here's a look at the racial backgrounds of Marylanders today. Maryland ranks sixth among all U.S. states with regard to African Americans as a percentage of the population.

Total population 5,296,486

White
3,391,308
64.0%

American Indian and Alaska Native
15,423
0.3%

Native Hawaiian and Other Pacific Islander
2,303
0.04%

Some other race
95,525
1.8%

Two or more races
103,587
2.0%

Asian
210,929
4.0%

Black or African American
1,477,411
27.9%

Note: 4.3% (227,916) of the population identify themselves as **Hispanic** or **Latino,** a cultural designation that crosses racial lines. Hispanics and Latinos are counted in this category as well as the racial category of their choice.

of European descent. Although small in numbers, Asians and Hispanics represent Maryland's fastest-growing groups, and the African-American population is growing steadily as well. Currently almost 60 percent of Baltimore's population is African American.

Maryland's median age is 36.0, which is relatively "old" in comparison with other highly populous states such as California and Texas. Maryland's median age, however, is only seven-tenths of a year higher than the national average (35.3 years).

Where Do Marylanders Live?

Approximately 80 percent of Maryland's people live in towns or cities with populations of 2,500 or more. The state's overall population density is quite high, with 542 people per square mile (209 per sq km) — significantly higher than the national average of 80 people per square mile (30 per sq km). More than 12 percent of the state's population lives in Baltimore, the state's largest city. Baltimore, however, has been losing population quickly since 1980, with a drop of

Educational Levels of Maryland Workers (age 25 and over)	
Less than 9th grade	246,505
9th to 12th grade, no diploma	427,427
High school graduate, including equivalency	878,432
Some college, no degree or associate degree	744,137
Bachelor's degree	486,695
Graduate or professional degree	339,469

▼ The skyline of Baltimore, Maryland's most populous city.

6.4 percent between 1980 and 1990, and an 11.5 percent decline during the next decade. Government-sponsored urban-renewal projects such as the Charles Center in midtown Baltimore — and similar projects in Rockville and Annapolis — are expected to start drawing people back to the urban centers.

Religion

Christianity is the predominant religion in Maryland. The various Christian denominations to which more than 80 percent of the population belongs include Baptists, Roman Catholics, and Methodists. There is also a significant Jewish presence in the state — approximately 4.7 percent of the population — whereas the national average is 1.7 percent. Approximately 0.2 percent of the population is Hindu, 0.2 percent Muslim, and 0.1 percent Buddhist, while 0.7 percent is agnostic (neither believing nor disbelieving in God).

Education

In its early days, colonial Maryland did not have an organized educational system. A few children, generally from wealthy families, received schooling from private tutors and church leaders. The colony levied funds for "free" schools in 1694. Two years later, King William's School opened its doors. King William's School was for boys only and educated a small number of poor students. It merged with the newly chartered St. John's College in 1784.

Throughout the first half of the nineteenth century, attempts were made to establish public schools in the state. The state constitution of 1864 set up a board of education and other offices, but it was not until the early twentieth century that a strong statewide public school system emerged. Before the U.S. Supreme Court outlawed racially segregated schools in 1954, Maryland had separate schools for African-American and white students, with most African-American schools receiving less funding and support than white schools. Within about twenty years of the Supreme Court ruling, most of the state's school systems were integrated. Today, all Maryland children are required to attend school between the ages of five and sixteen.

Higher Learning

Maryland is home to a great many respected universities and colleges. The University of Maryland has its main campus in College Park and branches in Baltimore, Princess Anne, and Adelphi.

Baltimore's Johns Hopkins University is Maryland's most prestigious private institution of higher learning. It is renowned for its School of Medicine, as well as for the Peabody Conservatory of Music. The United States Naval Academy *(above)* is located in Annapolis and is the revered alma mater of many of the nation's naval officers.

Bountiful Shores

> Here we were in the place I had so long been looking for. . . the counttry [sic] abounded with deer, bears, panthers, wolves, wild cats, catamounts, wild turkeys, foxes, rabbits, pheasants, partridges, wild bees, and in all the streams trout without number.
>
> — *Meshach Browning*, Forty-Four Years in the Life of a Hunter, *circa 1840*

The Chesapeake Bay divides Maryland into two sections: the Eastern and Western Shores. These regions' shorelines converge in Maryland's northeast corner. The low, marshy Eastern Shore is situated on the Delmarva Peninsula. (*Delmarva* is derived from the names of the three states that share the peninsula — *Del*aware, *Mar*yland, and Virginia, which is abbreviated as *VA*.) Along the Chesapeake Bay and Atlantic coast are a series of low, sandy barrier islands and vast stretches of swamps and tidal wetlands.

The Coastline

If Maryland's coastline is measured as a straight line, it covers 31 miles (50 km). If, however, the Chesapeake Bay's many inlets and arms are tracked, the state's coastline totals 3,190 miles (5,133 km). This meandering shoreline provides a wealth of wildlife habitats, as well as many excellent commercial and recreational harbors.

Highest Point

Backbone Mountain
3,360 ft (1,024 m)
above sea level

▼ *From left to right:* rolling cornfields in Baltimore County; a Maryland bluebird; Montgomery County stream; Crystal Grottoes Cavern in Washington County; farmland in Frederick County; Maryland rhododendrons in bloom.

Maryland's Rivers and Lakes

Most of Maryland's many rivers empty into the Chesapeake Bay. The Susquehanna River, which flows south from Pennsylvania into Maryland, is also a Chesapeake tributary. The Potomac River, which constitutes the state's southwestern boundary, widens into one of the Chesapeake's many arms. Maryland has no natural lakes, although many artificially created lakes and reservoirs exist, generally formed by hydroelectric dams. Another waterway is the Chesapeake and Delaware Canal, built in 1829. It connects the Chesapeake and Delaware Bays and allows goods to travel inland to the Delaware River.

Fields and Mountains

Fertile earth can be found all across the state, although Maryland's best agricultural soils are in the region known to geologists as the Piedmont, the area between the Blue Ridge Mountains and the Coastal Plain, as well as in certain well-drained Coastal Plain areas. Soils in the northerly Hagerstown Valley (or Great Valley) and western Maryland — used principally for livestock, dairy production, and fruit orchards — are of lesser quality. Forested lands also abound. About 35 percent of Maryland's land area is currently covered by trees.

The mountainous Blue Ridge region, named for the azure haze that often veils its peaks, runs from southern Pennsylvania to northern Georgia, reaching elevations within Maryland between 1,000 and 2,000 feet (305 and 610 m) near the Pennsylvania border. West of the Blue Ridge Mountains is the region known as the Appalachian Ridge and Valley. To the west of the valley, a series of forested ridges split Maryland from northeast to southwest, rising to nearly 2,000 feet (610 m) in places.

Average January temperature
Baltimore: 32°F (0°C)
Hagerstown: 30°F (-1°C)

Average July temperature
Baltimore: 77°F (25°C)
Hagerstown: 75°F (24°C)

Average yearly rainfall
Baltimore:
  20 inches (51 cm)
Hagerstown:
  20 inches (51 cm)

Average yearly snowfall
Baltimore:
  21 inches (54 cm)
Hagerstown:
  29 inches (74 cm)

Major Rivers

Susquehanna River
447 miles (719 km)

Potomac River
383 miles (616 km)

Youghiogheny River
135 miles (217 km)

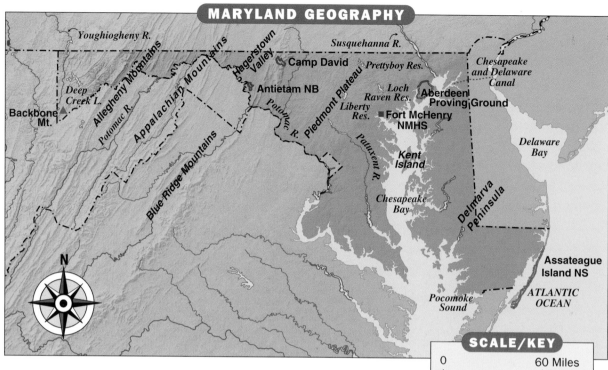

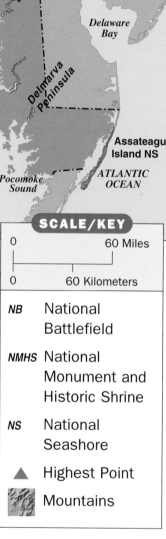

SCALE/KEY

0	60 Miles
0	60 Kilometers

NB National Battlefield

NMHS National Monument and Historic Shrine

NS National Seashore

▲ Highest Point

Mountains

The westernmost area of the state is part of the Appalachian Plateau, in which the Allegheny Mountains are the dominant geographical feature. It is here that Backbone Mountain, the state's highest point, is found.

Maryland's Climate

Maryland's climate is generally humid, with hot summers and mild winters. The state's mountainous northwest region tends to be cooler than the Atlantic coast or Chesapeake Bay areas. Maryland's annual precipitation (rain, snow, and other forms of moisture) averages about 43 inches (109 cm). Rain falls fairly evenly throughout the state. Maryland's climate varies more from east to west — and with increasing altitude — than it does from north to south. On July 3, 1898, Allegheny County set Maryland's record high temperature of 109° Fahrenheit (43° Celsius); that temperature was matched at Cumberland and Frederick on July 10, 1936. Oakland experienced the state's record low, -40°F (-40°C), on January 13, 1912.

Plants and Animals

Maryland boasts more than 150 species of trees, with oaks and hickories in greatest abundance. Ash, beech, maple, and tupelo are also commonly found throughout the state.

The lower Eastern Shore supports a southern pine forest, replete with loblolly, pitch, and Virginia pines. Azaleas, laurels, and rhododendrons number among the flowers growing at the edges of the woods. Maryland's official state flower, the black-eyed Susan, thrives along the Western Shore, as does a profusion of berries. The Eastern Shore supports grasslike plants called sedges.

Maryland's wildlife is a mixture of northern and southern species, including eastern cottontail rabbits, bluebirds, minks, opossums, orioles, raccoons, ravens, red and gray foxes, and white-tailed deer. Chipmunks, otters, squirrels, and woodchucks inhabit the north-central areas, while bears and bobcats are sometimes encountered in the mountains. Game birds such as partridge, quail, ruffed grouse, wild turkeys, and woodcocks are fixtures of the western Maryland uplands. Wild ducks and geese attract hunters on the Coastal Plain and the Eastern Shore, which lies along the Atlantic Flyway, a key migration route for waterfowl.

Maryland's coastal waters are havens for bluefish, crabs, diamondback terrapins, oysters, sea trout, shrimp, and striped bass. The cold rivers and streams of northern and western Maryland provide ideal habitats for freshwater trout, while carp, catfish, and suckers prefer the streams of the Piedmont and the Coastal Plain. The Chesapeake Bay supports a bounty of shellfish, including clams, crabs, and oysters, which have supported Maryland's fisheries.

Largest Lakes

Loch Raven Reservoir
37,958 acres
(15,361 ha)

Liberty Reservoir
29,805 acres
(12,061 ha)

Prettyboy Reservoir
18,541 acres (7,503 ha)

Deep Creek Lake
4,000 acres (1,619 ha)

▼ The Chesapeake Bay divides Maryland into two regions: the Eastern and Western Shores. The bay also provides Marylanders with boating opportunities.

A Secure and Optimistic Future

Our citizens enjoy enhanced security, and feel a renewed sense of optimism.
— *Governor Parris N. Glendening, 1998*

Colonial Maryland's economy was based on growing tobacco, which was often shipped out directly from each plantation's docks. After the Revolutionary War, Baltimore's seaport rose to prominence, rivaling the level of export activity at the Boston, New York, and Philadelphia ports. The construction of the Chesapeake and Ohio Canal and the Baltimore and Ohio Railroad in the 1800s allowed Maryland to forge commercial links with the Mississippi Valley and the nation's Midwest. The country's urgent need for goods during the Civil War and World Wars I and II transformed Baltimore into a center for shipbuilding and other industrial manufacturing.

Transportation

To accommodate its burgeoning post-World War II population, Maryland rebuilt its transportation system, establishing Baltimore's Friendship International Airport (now Baltimore-Washington International Airport) in 1950. The next thirteen years saw the completion of the Baltimore Harbor Tunnel and the Chesapeake Bay Bridge (now known as the William P. Lane, Jr., Memorial Bridge). Prior to the completion of the Chesapeake Bay Bridge, the Eastern Shore was accessible to the rest of the state only by boat or by long car trips.

◄ The Chesapeake Bay Bridge unites Maryland's Eastern and Western Shores.

DID YOU KNOW?

Greenbelt is home to the Goddard Space Flight Center. NASA develops many of its key space projects there.

Top Employers
(of workers age sixteen and over)

Services	35.2%
Wholesale and retail trade	18.8%
Public Administration	11.7%
Manufacturing	10.3%
Construction	7.9%
Finance, insurance, and real estate	7.4%
Transportation, communications, and public utilities	7.1%
Agriculture, forestry, and fisheries	1.5%
Mining	0.1%

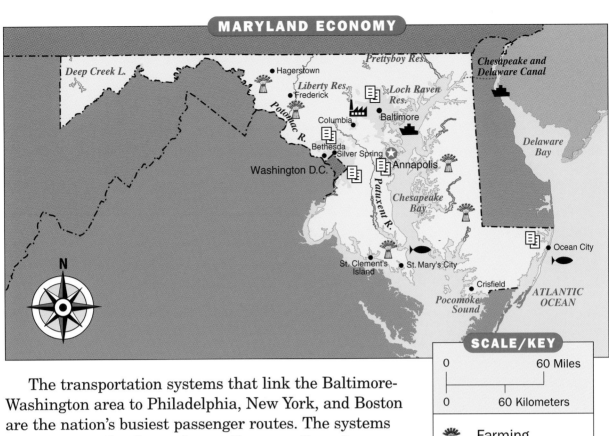

SCALE/KEY

0	60 Miles
0	60 Kilometers

🌾 Farming

🐟 Fishing

🏭 Manufacturing

📇 Services

⛴ Shipping

　 Urban Areas

The transportation systems that link the Baltimore-Washington area to Philadelphia, New York, and Boston are the nation's busiest passenger routes. The systems include air and rail travel as well as a section of Interstate 95, one of the nation's busiest highways.

Energy

Maryland's electricity comes from petroleum, natural gas, coal, nuclear power, and hydroelectric sources. About 60 percent of the state's electrical power is derived from coal-burning plants, while the state's two nuclear plants provide between 20 and 30 percent of the total.

Maryland Gross State Product　Millions of dollars

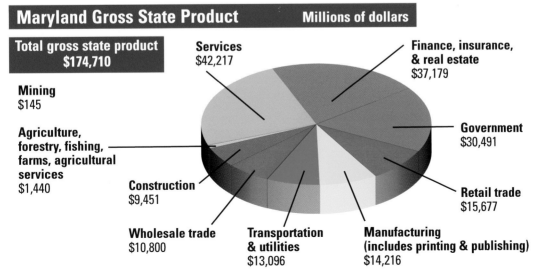

Total gross state product $174,710

Services $42,217

Finance, insurance, & real estate $37,179

Mining $145

Government $30,491

Agriculture, forestry, fishing, farms, agricultural services $1,440

Construction $9,451

Retail trade $15,677

Wholesale trade $10,800

Transportation & utilities $13,096

Manufacturing (includes printing & publishing) $14,216

Manufacturing and Mining

The manufacturing sector in Maryland today employs more than 250,000 people. Food products, electrical equipment, chemicals, transportation equipment, and printed materials are among the most economically important items created by Maryland's manufacturers.

The coal-mining region of Appalachia includes western Maryland. Maryland's coal production was at its peak in the early twentieth century but since then has declined, in part as a result of environmental concerns. The most important minerals now mined in Maryland are limestone, sand, and gravel, all essential to the construction industry. Maryland's clays and shales are key to the manufacture of bricks.

Agriculture

About one-third of the state's land is devoted to farming. Greenhouse and nursery plants and poultry are among the state's most profitable farm products. Other crops include soybeans, corn, hay, and wheat. Tobacco is cultivated in southern Maryland. Dairies and crop farming are important in the Piedmont region, while apples and peaches are specialties of western Maryland's valleys.

Service Sector

For decades, the growth of federal offices and activities spilled over into Maryland from the adjacent District of Columbia. As a result, federal government services make up a significant part of Maryland's economy. Many thousands of Marylanders are employed at such federal installations as the

▲ Plant sales from Maryland's nurseries and greenhouses generate more than $250 million annually.

Made in Maryland

Leading farm products and crops
Broiler chickens
Greenhouse products
Dairy products
Soybeans
Livestock
Feed crops (barley, corn, hay, oats)

Other products
Chemicals
Electrical equipment
Printed materials

Major Airport		
Airport	Location	Passengers per year (2000)
Baltimore/Washington International Airport	Baltimore/Washington	19,602,609

Aberdeen Proving Ground and Fort Detrick, as well as Andrews Air Force Base, the Goddard Space Flight Center, and Fort Meade (which includes the National Security Agency). The Social Security Administration and the National Institutes of Health are also headquartered in Maryland.

Other service-industry activities — such as schools, hospitals, retail enterprises, and the allied businesses of finance, insurance, and real estate — make crucial contributions to Maryland's economic well-being. Travel and tourism are also important, providing Marylanders with more than eighty-six thousand jobs. Ocean City, Maryland's largest resort town, draws more than four million visitors each summer. Baltimore's Inner Harbor area attracts nearly five million visitors annually.

Fishing

Commercial fishing has been a critically important activity for generations. Much of the state's fishing is carried out by a fleet of wind-powered vessels called skipjacks. By law all oysters must be harvested by sail-powered boats, both to fight pollution and conserve oysters. During recent years, however, the populations of crabs, clams, and oysters have declined because of pollution in the Chesapeake Bay. This pollution is principally caused by fertilizer runoff from farms, as well as industrial wastes generated in the cities. In 1985, Maryland's government initiated an extensive clean up of the bay, an effort that is expected to continue past the year 2010. Neighboring states Pennsylvania, Virginia, and Delaware — as well as Washington, D.C. — have partnered with Maryland in this ambitious project.

Spice of Life

In 1938, Gustav Brunn fled Nazi Germany and settled in Baltimore. Brunn had worked in the spice business, so he got a job at the McCormick Spice Factory. Brunn was fired after just a few days. Later, he formed his own company and created a seasoning mix to complement steamed crabs, Maryland's signature dish. He named the seasoning Old Bay after a steamship line that traveled between Baltimore and Virginia.

▼ Baltimore's Inner Harbor is both a busy seaport and a tourist destination.

Preserving Liberty

> Think, Oh! my Countrymen, to what Men become subjected when their *Liberties* are lost. Learn to value your own, and teach your Children to do the same, beyond Fortune or even Life.
>
> — The Maryland Gazette, *May 12, 1768*

Maryland's charter established a representative assembly that first met in 1635, but the assembly members did not have much power. The colony's proprietor, Cecilius Calvert, could veto the assembly's actions. Meanwhile, Leonard Calvert, Maryland's first colonial governor, controlled a council that functioned separately from the assembly. It reserved the right to review, and sometimes nullify, any laws the assembly passed. This system guaranteed bitter political infighting, made worse by land disputes and arguments over political appointments made by the Calvert brothers.

During the colonial period — the 1600s and 1700s — a patronage system existed in Maryland. It ensured that the best land and the choicest political appointments went to those most favored by the colony's proprietor, or patron. Unhappiness with the colonial proprietorship system became acute in the 1760s and put Maryland on a course that would lead it to join the other rebellious colonies in the Revolutionary War.

The Maryland Constitution

Maryland adopted its first constitution on November 8, 1776. It remained in force until 1851, when a second constitution was adopted. In 1864, while the Civil War still raged, Maryland adopted a third constitution that prohibited slavery and penalized Marylanders who had supported the Confederacy. Three years later Maryland adopted a fourth constitution, which was somewhat more lenient toward former Confederates. This constitution

State Constitution

The parliament of Great Britain, by a declaratory act, having assumed a right to make laws to bind the Colonies in all cases whatsoever, and, in pursuance of Rich claim, endeavoured, by force of arms, to subjugate the United Colonies to an unconditional submission to their will and power, and having at length constrained them to declare themselves independent States, and to assume government under the authority of the people; Therefore we, the Delegates of Maryland, in free and full Convention assembled, taking into our most serious consideration the best means of establishing a good Constitution in this State, for the sure foundation and more permanent security thereof.

— *from Maryland Constitution, 1776*

Elected Posts in the Executive Branch		
Office	Length of Term	Term Limits
Governor	4 years	2 consecutive terms
Lieutenant Governor	4 years	none
Comptroller	4 years	none
State Treasurer	4 years	none
Attorney General	4 years	none

DID YOU KNOW?

In 1861, when southern states began to secede from the Union, a majority of the Maryland legislature refused to even consider voting on the question of secession, saving the U.S. capital from being trapped between their state and its other southern neighbors.

remains in effect today. It divides Maryland's government into three branches: executive, legislative, and judicial.

Maryland's constitution may still be amended either by the state legislature or by a constitutional convention. Amendments that are proposed by the legislature must gain the approval of a three-fifths majority of both legislative houses, as well as a simple majority of Maryland voters. Maryland voters must approve amendments proposed at constitutional conventions.

▼ **The Maryland State House is the oldest legislative building in any state that is still in use.**

The Executive Branch

Maryland's governor is the state's chief executive officer and serves a four-year term. A governor may serve an unlimited number of terms, but no governor may serve more than two terms consecutively. The voters also elect the state's lieutenant governor, attorney general, treasurer, and comptroller.

Other executive-branch offices, such as the secretary of state, the adjutant general (who commands the more than nine thousand National Guard troops in the state), and most members of state boards, are appointed by the governor. The governor has the authority to fill many judicial posts. He or she can appoint the judges to the state's appellate courts, circuit courts, and district courts.

The Legislative Branch

During the post-Civil War decades, political power shifted away from the state's executive branch, and the influence of the state legislature increased. Known as the General Assembly, Maryland's legislature consists of a senate, with forty-seven members, and a house of delegates, with 141 members.

Maryland's forty-seven legislative districts each elect one senator and three delegates, all of whom serve four-year terms. General Assembly sessions begin on the second Wednesday in January and are required to conclude ninety days later. The governor may also convene special sessions of the General Assembly; he or she must do so if a majority of the members of both houses sign a special petition for that purpose.

The Judicial Branch

Maryland's highest court is called the court of appeals. It consists of seven judges, one each from the state's seven judicial districts (called "circuits"). These judges are initially appointed by the governor, subject to state senate confirmation. Following a term of at least one year, each judge must be approved by the voters. If approved, the judge serves a ten-year term. The chief judge of the court is appointed by the governor. He or she also serves as the head of the state's judicial branch. As its name suggests, the court of appeals hears cases that are appeals of decisions made by lower courts, usually the court of special appeals. It is also the only court in which appeals of death penalty cases are heard.

The court of special appeals has twelve associate judges and one chief judge, designated by the governor. They are appointed, subject to voter approval, in the same manner as the judges of the court of appeals. This court usually hears appeals of decisions in both civil and criminal cases made by the circuit courts or a special court that disposes of estates.

Both civil and criminal trials may be held in Maryland's circuit courts. There are eight circuits, composed of groups of counties and the city of Baltimore. The total number of circuit court judges is 146, with a chief judge who is chosen based on length of service on the court. These judges are appointed and elected in the same way as the appellate court judges, except that they serve fifteen-year terms.

The Act of Religious Toleration of 1649

The Calvert family, who were at the time Roman Catholics, instituted the 1649 Act of Religious Toleration, in part to reassure England's Puritan-led government that Protestants in Maryland would not be persecuted. This law protected only Christian faiths; non-Christian faiths were frowned upon. In 1660, when Puritans lost control of the English government, representatives of England's new government began to persecute Puritans in several colonies. Many Puritans fled to Maryland, then still under the proprietorship of Cecilius Calvert. The Act of Religious Toleration allowed them to worship freely.

General Assembly			
House	Number of Members	Length of Term	Term Limits
Senate	47 senators	4 years	none
House of Delegates	141 delegates	4 years	none

Other courts in Maryland include the district court, which hears less serious criminal cases and civil cases where smaller amounts of money are at stake. There are no jury trials in this court. The orphans' court hears cases having to do with wills and the administration of the assets of minors who do not have living parents.

Local Government

Maryland's local governments follow several models. More than half of Maryland's twenty-three counties are governed by either county commissioners or elected governing boards, which blend the functions of executive and legislative branches of government. The remaining counties are governed by county councils, county executives, or a combination of both.

Baltimore, not being part of any county but designated as an "independent city," is governed by a mayor, an eighteen-member city council, and a council president. Maryland's counties are permitted to adopt either of two forms of home rule, both of which allow county governments to operate independently of the direct oversight of the state legislature most of the time. Thirteen of Maryland's counties have adopted home rule, as have the state's incorporated cities.

National Government

Maryland sends two senators and eight representatives to the U.S. Congress and has ten votes in the electoral college. The state has been solidly Democratic for most of the twentieth century. Because of this, primary elections are often more important to voters than are general elections. Republicans tend to do best with voters in the northeastern part of the state and in the suburbs. Maryland elected its first African-American congressman, Parren Mitchell, in 1970. Mitchell was also the first African American to receive a degree from the University of Maryland graduate school, after suing the school to admit him in 1950. The state elected its first woman senator, Barbara Mikulski, in 1986. Mikulski had served in the U.S. House of Representatives, making her the first woman ever to hold seats in both houses. Mikulski was also the first woman to win a statewide election in Maryland.

Rise and Fall of Spiro Agnew

The first Marylander to hold high national office, Spiro T. Agnew (1918-1996) was elected Vice President of the United States in 1968 and 1972. Agnew got his political start as chief executive for Baltimore County in 1962, then swiftly ascended to Maryland's governorship. Once proclaimed in a national poll as one of the country's three most admired men, Agnew soiled his reputation by accepting bribes and evading income taxes, for which he was convicted in 1973. Agnew resigned his office on October 10, 1973.

Sound and Comfortable Living

> Of the external embellishments of life we have plenty . . . But we have something much better: we have a tradition of sound and comfortable living.
>
> — *H. L. Mencken, journalist, in a 1931* Baltimore Evening Sun *column*

Marylanders greatly value their cultural, creative, and leisure pursuits. The state has produced and nurtured dozens of world-class authors, musicians, and athletes, catering to a variety of tastes and interests as wide and all-inclusive as the United States.

The Lively Arts

Maryland's cultural center for orchestral music, opera, dance, and theater is Baltimore. The Baltimore Symphony Orchestra makes its home in the Joseph Meyerhoff Symphony Hall, which is renowned for its acoustics. The Lyric Opera House is home to the Baltimore Opera Company, and public concerts are frequently held in the Inner Harbor's outdoor arena, the Baltimore Arena, and the Peabody Conservatory of Music.

The Maryland Hall for the Creative Arts serves Maryland's capital, Annapolis, and is a venue for ballet, classical music, and opera. Other important Maryland concert, theater, and dance performance centers include the Weinberg Center for the Arts in Frederick and the Cumberland Theater in Cumberland.

▼ Billie Holiday, a Baltimore native, is regarded as one of the finest jazz vocalists of the twentieth century.

Maryland has produced several world-famous jazz musicians. Among the best known are Baltimore natives Chick Webb (a bandleader of the 1930s and 1940s), harmonica player Larry Adler, composer and pianist James Hubert "Eubie" Blake, and legendary singer Billie Holiday. Grammy-winning singer Toni Braxton grew up in Severn.

Museums

One of the most interesting museums in Maryland is Baltimore's American Visionary Art Museum. This museum is dedicated to the works of so-called "outsider artists," self-taught artists who live and work on the margins of mainstream society and whose work is not usually displayed in galleries and museums.

The Baltimore Museum of Art emphasizes paintings, prints, and sculptures and boasts the largest collection of paintings by the French artist Henri Matisse in any public gallery. The Maryland Historical Society in Baltimore has Francis Scott Key's original manuscript of "The Star-Spangled Banner." The society's collections include Empire furniture, miniatures, glass, jewelry, and lace. Other important museums include the U.S. Naval Academy Museum and the Maryland State Archives Museum, both in Annapolis, and Baltimore's Walters Art Gallery. It seems that one could spend a lifetime sampling the Old Line State's cultural wonders — and still not have sufficient time to experience them all.

Art and Architecture

Maryland has been a strong center for the visual arts since the eighteenth century. Between 1708 and 1717, German painter Justus Englehardt Kuhn worked in Annapolis. He was one of the first artists to render the image of a slave.

The First Washington Monument

Baltimore has long been famous for its many monuments and historic landmarks. President John Quincy Adams dubbed it the "Monumental City." Among those honored are President George Washington, Supreme Court Justice Thurgood Marshall, and the troops who defended the city during the War of 1812. Pictured above is architect Robert Mills's first Washington Monument. He later designed the Washington Monument that stands in Washington, D.C.

Later in the century, Chestertown native Charles Willson Peale gained fame for his portraits of Presidents George Washington and Thomas Jefferson.

French architect Maximilian Godefroy moved to Baltimore in 1805 and designed the city's famous Battle Monument. Godefroy also designed Baltimore's Merchant's Exchange Building, as well as several churches. Architect Robert Mills, who made his home in Baltimore in 1815, designed two Washington Monuments — one in Baltimore, as well as the more famous one in the nation's capital. Maryland is also well known for a form of sculptural folk art: the wooden decoys used by Chesapeake Bay hunters to attract ducks and geese. Over the centuries, the carving and painting of these decoys has become a specialty of highly skilled artists. Some of the best examples are on display at the Havre de Grace Decoy Museum.

Literature

Maryland's literary tradition extends back to the seventeenth century, when Father Andrew White wrote a contemporary account of the colony's founding called *A Briefe Relation of the Voyage unto Maryland*. Mason Locke Weems, a minister from Maryland, wrote a highly complimentary biography of George Washington, which was the source of the myth that a youthful Washington chopped down a cherry tree — and confessed to the deed uttering the famous lines, "I cannot tell a lie. I did it with my little axe." Weems invented the entire story.

Edgar Allan Poe is probably Maryland's most famous nineteenth-century literary son. Poe, who lived in Baltimore, authored eerie stories such as "The Tell-Tale Heart" and "The Fall

The Banneker-Douglass Museum in Annapolis is housed in what was once the Mount Moriah African Methodist Episcopal Church. The museum is the state's official collection of material related to African-American history.

of the House of Usher" and the poem "The Raven." Escaped slave and abolitionist Frederick Douglass, who was born in Tuckahoe, gained fame first for his speeches. Then, in 1845, he wrote his autobiography, *Narrative of the Life of Frederick Douglass, An American Slave,* in part because his eloquence had convinced some people that he had never been a slave at all.

Twentieth-century Maryland produced writers such as Baltimore-based H. L. Mencken, whose newspaper columns often skewered the behavior and attitudes of his countrymen. The humorous poet Ogden Nash, who also resided in Baltimore, produced numerous volumes of light verse as well as children's books. Other writers with strong Maryland ties include novelists John Barth, Tom Clancy, Dashiell Hammett, and Anne Tyler. A native of Cambridge, John Barth often sets his works in Eastern Shore locations. Novelist Tom Clancy, born in Baltimore, writes thrillers such as *The Hunt for Red October* (1984). Several have been turned into major motion pictures. Dashiell Hammet was a mystery writer, most famous for his *Thin Man* series, which was turned into six popular movies in the 1930s and 1940s. Anne Tyler is a long-time Baltimore resident who has used that city as the backdrop for many of her books.

▲ Edgar Allan Poe is regarded as the first American mystery writer.

Maryland Outdoors

Maryland's varied terrain gives residents and visitors a wealth of recreational opportunities. Forests, lakes, and coastline beaches are all available for activities and relaxation. In the winter, skiers can enjoy the snowy slopes in Garrett County, while in the summer, fishing boats fill the Chesapeake Bay and crab pots bring up the state's favorite meal.

Maryland has forty-seven state parks and forests, covering more than 90,000 acres (36,423 ha). Janes Island State Park in the Chesapeake consists of one section that can be reached by car and another that can only be reached by boat. Each year the park hosts a "Power Paddle" race for kayakers and canoeists through the park's marshland waterways.

A Mother of Invention

Baltimore native Frank Vincent Zappa (1940–1993), innovative composer, guitarist, and satirist, originated the musical genre known as "freak rock." He was also one of the first to blend rock music with classical and jazz. He founded a band called the Mothers of Invention in 1964 and recorded more than fifty-five albums. His first album, *Freak Out,* may have inspired the Beatles' famous 1967 album, *Sergeant Pepper's Lonely Hearts Club Band.*

At Rocks State Park, huge boulders are piled into strange natural formations. The Susquehannock used to gather for sacred ceremonies at the King and Queen Seat, a 190-foot (58-m) rocky outcrop on the banks of Deer Creek.

A 2,898-foot (883-m) peak in Dans Mountain State Park provides panoramic views of the surrounding country. The cliffs along the shoreline at Calvert Cliffs State Park were formed fifteen million years ago and have yielded fossils of more than six hundred species. Visitors can hunt for fossils along the beach or hike through the woods farther inland.

Among Maryland's historic parks is Antietam National Battlefield. On this field, in September 1862, more men were killed than on any other single day of the Civil War. The site is now a park, which visitors may tour by foot, car, bicycle, or horse. In Glen Echo, at the Clara Barton National Historic Site, visitors can tour the house where Clara Barton, famed Civil War nurse, lived and where the American Red Cross, which she directed, was headquartered. The Hampton

Baltimore Sports Monuments

Babe Ruth Birthplace and Museum: Open April through October (baseball season), this museum — housed in the brick building in which Babe Ruth was born — is dedicated to the life of baseball's immortal Baltimore-born slugger.

Lacrosse Hall of Fame & Museum: This museum celebrates the popular Native American–invented sport.

Sport	Team	Home
Baseball	Baltimore Orioles	Oriole Park at Camden Yards
Football	Baltimore Ravens	PSINet Stadium

▼ Point Given breaks through the field to finish first at the 126th running of the Preakness in 2001.

National Historic Site in Towson features an elegant mansion built in 1790 for a wealthy merchant's family. It was the largest house in the United States at the time. Tours provide a glimpse back into the everyday life of Marylanders — including African-American slaves and white household servants as well as property owners — in the late eighteenth century.

Sports

Baseball is a favorite Maryland pastime. In 1954, the St. Louis Browns moved to Baltimore and became the Orioles. The "Baltimore chop," in which a ball is deliberately driven into the ground in front of home plate to produce a high, hard-to-catch bounce, is a Maryland invention. Cal Ripken, Jr., and pioneering African-American player and manager Frank Robinson both played for the Orioles, as did fellow Hall-of-Famers Jim Palmer and Brooks Robinson. Legendary New York Yankees slugger George Herman "Babe" Ruth was born in Baltimore. That city's Oriole Park at Camden Yards — a stadium built expressly for big-league baseball — stands on a site where Ruth played ball as a boy.

The Baltimore Colts recruited a number of distinguished football players during the team's lengthy history, including running back Lenny Moore and quarterback Johnny Unitas. The Colts won the 1971 Super Bowl. They relocated to Indianapolis, Indiana, in 1984. Twelve years later, however, Baltimore again became home to a professional football team when the Cleveland Browns (now the Ravens) relocated there. The Ravens won the Super Bowl in 2001. They take their name from Edgar Allan Poe's famous poem "The Raven."

Horse racing is a Maryland tradition dating back to the eighteenth century. One of the sport's most important annual events is the Preakness, the second part of the Triple Crown. It began and is run at Pimlico Race Track in Baltimore. The race takes its name from a horse called Preakness that won the inaugural race at Pimlico in 1870. The Maryland Jockey Club named a race instituted in 1873 in the horse's honor.

Memorable Marylanders

The formation of a national character... depends on the lofty and commanding stand to be taken by the genius of American literature; on the advances made by American poets, sculptors, painters, orators, legislators in celebrating American action, scenery, etc.

— Baltimore Morning Chronicle, *1821*

Following are only a few of the thousands of people who were born, died, or spent much of their lives in Maryland and made extraordinary contributions to the state and the nation.

JOHNS HOPKINS
PHILANTHROPIST

BORN: *May 19, 1795, Anne Arundel County*
DIED: *December 24, 1873, Baltimore*

Johns Hopkins began working as a commission merchant in Baltimore at the age of seventeen. In 1819, Hopkins opened his own firm, later called Hopkins Brothers. The firm set up grocery wholesale operations in Maryland, Virginia, and North Carolina. Hopkins played an important part in establishing the Baltimore and Ohio Railroad and joined its board of directors in 1847, the year he retired from his firm. Although extremely wealthy, Hopkins lived frugally, once refusing to carpet his home because he preferred to keep his money in the bank. With others, however, he could be extremely generous. He loaned significant amounts of money to the city of Baltimore during the Civil War and during a financial panic that took place in 1873. Hopkins also used his immense wealth to provide Baltimore with several enduring gifts, including land for a public park and funds to establish the Johns Hopkins University and Johns Hopkins Hospital.

EDGAR ALLAN POE
AUTHOR

BORN: *January 19, 1809, Boston, MA*
DIED: *October 7, 1849, Baltimore*

Edgar Allan Poe was known in his day for poetry and literary criticism, but today he is best remembered for his eerie fiction. Poe began writing poetry when he was a young man, publishing his first book of verse, *Tamerlane and Other Poems,* in 1827. In 1829, he moved to Baltimore to live with his aunt Maria Clemm and, two years later, married her daughter, his cousin Virginia. He published about fifty poems, the most famous of which was "The Raven" (1845). A pioneer of the short story, Poe wrote such terrifying tales as "The Pit and the Pendulum" (1842) and "The Tell-Tale Heart" (1843). Other short stories include "The Murders in the Rue Morgue" (1841), which is credited by some as the first detective story. In 1849, Poe died of what was believed to be alcohol poisoning. A recent theory based on the symptoms he suffered before his death suggests that he may, in fact, have died of rabies.

FREDERICK DOUGLASS
ABOLITIONIST

BORN: *circa February 1817, Tuckahoe*
DIED: *February 20, 1895, Washington, D.C.*

African-American abolitionist Frederick Augustus Washington Bailey was born a slave. As a boy he was sent to work in Baltimore, where he learned to read and write and where he first heard of the abolition movement. After several years in Baltimore, he was returned to the country to work on a farm, where he was brutally treated. He escaped in 1838 and made his way to New Bedford, Massachusetts, changing his name to Frederick Douglass. In Massachusetts Douglass became involved in the antislavery movement and so impressed William Lloyd Garrison and others that he was invited to become a speaker for the Anti-Slavery Society. In 1845, he published his autobiography, *Narrative of the Life of Frederick Douglass, An American Slave,* in which he described the hardships and injustices he had suffered. Because slavery had not yet been abolished, Douglass put himself at risk of being recaptured by publishing this book. In

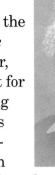

1847, Douglass started the abolitionist journal *The North Star* in Rochester, New York, and edited it for seventeen years. During the Civil War, Douglass worked to help African-American men enlist in the Union Army and also advised President Abraham Lincoln on race relations. After the war, Douglass continued to work to better the lives of African Americans and to help U.S. women secure the right to vote.

HARRIET TUBMAN
ABOLITIONIST

BORN: *circa 1820, Dorchester County*
DIED: *March 10, 1913, Auburn, NY*

Harriet Tubman was a runaway slave and abolitionist who became a key "conductor" on the Underground Railroad, which helped free hundreds of slaves. Born to slave parents, Tubman escaped in 1849 and made her way north to freedom. She secretly returned to Southern slave states many times during the 1850s, at great personal risk, to lead some three hundred slaves — including her parents — to freedom. When her fellow fugitives sometimes became panicky or tired, Tubman kept them moving by brandishing a gun. During the Civil War, Tubman served the Union as an army cook, a nurse, and a spy. After the war, she ran a home for poor and elderly African Americans in Auburn, New York. Tubman was buried with full military honors.

H. L. MENCKEN
JOURNALIST, EDITOR, AND CRITIC

BORN: *September 12, 1880, Baltimore*
DIED: *January 29, 1956, Baltimore*

Henry Louis Mencken was one of the most influential U.S. editors, essayists, and social critics of the first half of the twentieth century. From 1924 to 1933, when he edited the *American Mercury*, Mencken exposed his readers to new U.S. writers, such as Theodore Dreiser, James Branch Cabell, and Sinclair Lewis. Born to a middle-class German-American family, Mencken got his first job at age eighteen on the *Baltimore Morning Herald*. Seven years later he became the editor of the *Evening Herald* and began writing controversial, sarcastic columns for the *Baltimore Evening Sun*. In 1914, he gained national prominence as a coeditor of *Smart Set,* producing essays that criticized U.S. culture, education, religion, and politics. One of Mencken's most memorable quotes is: "The great artists of the world are never Puritans, and seldom even ordinarily respectable."

"EUBIE" BLAKE
JAZZ PIANIST AND COMPOSER

BORN: *February 7, 1883, Baltimore*
DIED: *February 12, 1983, New York, NY*

A ragtime pianist, James Hubert Blake had a long and distinguished career as a popular composer. With his longtime partner, songwriter Noble Sissle, Blake wrote the musical *Shuffle Along* (1921), which became Broadway's most successful African American–created show up to that time. Two of Blake's songs from this show —

"I'm Just Wild About Harry" and "Memories of You" — are still performed regularly. Blake was "rediscovered" in 1969, when the album *The Eighty-Six Years of Eubie Blake* was released. Blake later established his own record company and made a biographical film. His life and music were honored in the hit 1978 Broadway musical *Eubie.* Blake, who lived to be one hundred, is famous for saying, "If I'd known I was going to live this long, I'd have taken better care of myself."

"BABE" RUTH
BASEBALL PLAYER

BORN: *February 6, 1895, Baltimore*
DIED: *August 16, 1948, New York, NY*

George Herman Ruth was one of baseball's greatest hitters and arguably the game's most famous player in the 1920s and early 1930s. Ruth began playing in the major leagues in 1914 as a left-handed pitcher for the Boston Red Sox. He won 89 of the 158 games he pitched between 1914 and 1919. In 1920, he was sold to the New York Yankees, where Ruth gained his true fame as a hitter, earning the nickname "the Sultan of Swat." Ruth led the league in home runs a record twelve times, with fifty-nine homers in 1921 and a then-record sixty in 1927. He

retired in 1935 with 714 career home runs, a record that remained intact until Henry Aaron broke it 1974. Ruth was a charter member of the Baseball Hall of Fame in 1936.

THURGOOD MARSHALL
JURIST

BORN: *July 2, 1908, Baltimore*
DIED: *January 24, 1993, Bethesda*

Thurgood Marshall was the first African American to serve on the U.S. Supreme Court. Impressed by Marshall's abilities as an advocate in civil rights cases, especially the 1954 school-desegregation case *Brown v. Board of Education of Topeka*, President John F. Kennedy appointed Marshall to the Federal Court of Appeals for the Second Circuit in 1961. Four years later, Marshall became the first African-American U.S. solicitor general. In 1967, President Lyndon Johnson nominated him to the U.S. Supreme Court. Memorials in Annapolis and Baltimore now stand in his honor.

BILLIE HOLIDAY
JAZZ SINGER

BORN: *April 7, 1915, Baltimore*
DIED: *July 17, 1959, New York, NY*

Born Eleanora Fagan Gough, Billie Holiday, often called "Lady Day," is widely regarded as the finest vocalist to emerge from the 1930s jazz era. A poor child, she grew up in Baltimore listening to recordings of Louis Armstrong and Bessie Smith. After she and her mother moved from Baltimore to New York City, Holiday worked in small Harlem nightclubs, where she developed her distinctive singing style. She later recorded with Duke Ellington, Benny Goodman, and pianist Teddy Wilson. Among Holiday's most noteworthy recordings are "Strange Fruit" (released in 1939), which tells the story of a lynching in the South, and Holiday's own composition "God Bless the Child" (1941), which deals with poverty. Through much of her career, Holiday struggled against drug addiction, which took her life at the age of forty-four.

CAL RIPKEN, JR.
BASEBALL PLAYER

BORN: *August 24, 1960, Havre de Grace*

Calvin Edwin Ripken, Jr., whose father was a Baltimore Orioles coach from 1976 to 1992, grew up around baseball. He began playing with the Orioles in 1981 and was voted American League Rookie of the Year in 1982. Ripken, who played shortstop, was twice named the American League's Most Valuable Player (1983 and 1991) and twice received the Golden Glove Award for excellence in fielding (1991 and 1992). In 1992, he received the Roberto Clemente Award, which is presented annually to the player who best exemplifies the game of baseball both on and off the field. Ripken played in 2,632 consecutive games, surpassing Lou Gehrig's record of 2,130 games. He retired from the game on October 6, 2001. After retiring, Ripken became involved in youth baseball. Despite his record-setting career, he has said, "I never perceive of myself as a hero of any kind. I'm just a baseball player."

Maryland
History At-A-Glance

1524
Giovanni da Verrazano is the first European to see the Chesapeake Bay as he explores the coast of Maryland.

1572
Pedro Menéndez de Avilés of Spain enters the Chesapeake Bay.

1608
Captain John Smith explores and maps the Chesapeake Bay.

1631
William Claiborne sets up a trading post on Kent Island.

1632
England's King Charles I grants the official charter for the Maryland colony to Lord Baltimore.

1634
The first European settlers reach the Chesapeake Bay.

1649
Maryland's colonial assembly approves the religious toleration law.

1696
Maryland's first free school opens in Annapolis.

1767
Charles Mason and Jeremiah Dixon finish surveying the Maryland-Pennsylvania border, creating the Mason-Dixon Line.

1780
Maryland's State House holds its first session.

1788
On April 28, Maryland ratifies the U.S. Constitution and becomes the seventh state to enter the Union.

1791
Maryland contributes the land that will become Washington, D.C., the nation's capital.

1600   **1700**   **1800**

1492
Christopher Columbus comes to New World.

1607
Capt. John Smith and three ships land on Virginia coast and start first English settlement in New World — Jamestown.

1754–63
French and Indian War.

1773
Boston Tea Party.

1776
Declaration of Independence adopted July 4.

1777
Articles of Confederation adopted by Continental Congress.

1787
U.S. Constitution written.

1812–14
War of 1812.

United States
History At-A-Glance

1814
Francis Scott Key, an eyewitness to the British invasion of Baltimore, writes "The Star-Spangled Banner."

1830
The first U.S. steam locomotive, *Tom Thumb*, begins running between Baltimore and Ellicott's Mills.

1844
Telegraph messages are sent along the first U.S. telegraph line, which connects Baltimore and Washington, D.C.

1858
The fossil teeth of a sauropod dinosaur are discovered near Muirkirk.

1861
Maryland, a slave state, chooses not to secede from the Union.

1864
Maryland adopts a constitution that abolishes slavery.

1867
Maryland adopts its fourth constitution, a document that is still in use today.

1919–33
Maryland defies federal Prohibition laws and comes to be known as the "Free State."

1952
The Chesapeake Bay Bridge opens, connecting Maryland's Eastern and Western Shores.

1954
Baltimore desegregates its public schools.

1967
Thurgood Marshall of Baltimore becomes the first African-American U.S. Supreme Court justice.

1985
Maryland and other nearby states begin cleaning up the polluted Chesapeake Bay.

1800 — **1900** — **2000**

1848
Gold discovered in California draws eighty thousand prospectors in the 1849 Gold Rush.

1861–65
Civil War.

1869
Transcontinental railroad completed.

1917–18
U.S. involvement in World War I.

1929
Stock market crash ushers in Great Depression.

1941–45
U.S. involvement in World War II.

1950–53
U.S. fights in the Korean War.

1964–73
U.S. involvement in Vietnam War.

2000
George W. Bush wins the closest presidential election in history.

2001
A terrorist attack in which four hijacked airliners crash into New York City's World Trade Center, the Pentagon, and farmland in western Pennsylvania leaves thousands dead or injured.

▼ **The Western Maryland Railroad's Port Covington Yards, circa 1913.**

Festivals and Fun for All

Check web site for exact date and directions.

Antietam National Battlefield, Sharpsburg

Each December, a Memorial Illumination honors soldiers who fell at the site of one of the bloodiest battles of the Civil War. Here, Union forces turned back the first Confederate invasion of the North on September 17, 1862.

www.nps.gov/anti

Artscape, Baltimore

In mid-July, Baltimore's artists, poets, and pottery-makers take over the downtown sidewalks and offer their wares for sale. Events include hat-making, musical performances, and dramatic readings from the works of Edgar Allan Poe.

www.artscape.org

Assateague Island National Seashore, Assateague Island

This camping, picnicking, hiking, and fishing destination is famous for its wild ponies. According to legend, the ponies' ancestors were survivors of a sixteenth-century Spanish shipwreck. They are more likely descended from ponies hidden on the island by their tax-dodging seventeenth-century owners. Two-thirds of the island is Maryland's property; the remainder belongs to Virginia.

www.nps.gov/asis

Autumn Glory Festival, Deep Creek

In mid-October, Marylanders gather in Garrett County to celebrate the fall foliage in all its splendor. This event boasts parades, bands, arts and crafts, and more.

www.haleyfarm.com/deep-creek-md-events.html

Commissioning Week at the U.S. Naval Academy, Annapolis

Each year at the end of May, the graduates of the U.S. Naval Academy in Annapolis receive their commissions as military officers. Some of the ceremonies and events are open to the public.

www.usna.com

Deal Island Skipjack Races, Deal Island

Every Labor Day weekend, boaters gather from all over the Chesapeake region to compete in races.

www.baydreaming.com/dealisland.htm

Defenders Day Celebration, Baltimore

Fort McHenry's bombardment by the British in 1814, during the War of 1812, and Francis Scott Key's writing of "The Star-Spangled Banner" are commemorated each September during the Defenders Day festivities, which include a historic presentation and a picnic for honeymoon couples.

www.bcpl.net/~jhade/defend.html

Flag Day Ceremonies at Fort McHenry, Baltimore

Every June 14 (Flag Day), historic Fort McHenry hosts a thrilling jet flyover, a 21-gun salute from the Fort McHenry Guard, a band concert, and a dramatic fireworks display.
www.bcpl.net/~etowner/flagday.html

Maryland State Fair, Timonium

The Maryland State Fair celebrates Maryland agriculture, animal husbandry, and crafts. Hot-air balloon demonstrations, live music, and horse races are part of the fun.
www.marylandstatefair.com

National Hard Crab Derby, Crisfield

Crisfield's Somers Cove Marina comes alive each Labor Day weekend with a wealth of events, including crab races, a parade, boat races, and a crab-picking contest.
www.crisfield.org/eventindex.cfm

Preakness Celebration, Baltimore

Held on the third Saturday of May at Pimlico Race Course, the Preakness Celebration offers a series of public events, including hot-air balloon rides, block parties, parades, and more. The Preakness Stakes, a famous horse race, is the second event in thoroughbred racing's Triple Crown.
www.preaknesscelebration.org

Strawberry Festival, Sandy Spring

In early June the Sandy Spring Museum hosts an event that includes entertainment, crafts, museum exhibits, food, games, and, of course, strawberries.
www.sandyspringmuseum.com/f420.html

Takoma Park Folk Festival, Takoma Park

For twenty-five years, Takoma Park has been welcoming musicians, dancers, and craftspeople each September for a celebration of folk culture. The festival raises money to support local youth organizations.
www.tpff.org

Towsontown Spring Festival, Towson

Towson welcomes visitors to its annual festival in early May. The festival features performances on five stages, as well as an art contest and a classic car show.
www.towsontownspringfestival.com

Waterfowl Festival, Easton

Held each November in historic Easton, the festival features art, hunting decoys, children's activities, food, and music.
www.waterfowlfestival.org

Books

Arthur, Joe. *The Story of Thurgood Marshall: Justice for All. Famous Lives.* Milwaukee, WI: Gareth Stevens, 1996. Learn about the life and career of this famous Baltimore judge, who served on the U.S. Supreme Court.

Bell, David Owen. *Awesome Chesapeake; A Kid's Guide to the Bay.* Centreville, MD: Tidewater Publishers, 1994. A guide to the complex ecology of Chesapeake Bay.

Fradin, Dennis Brindell. *The Maryland Colony.* Danbury, CT: Children's Press, 1990. A detailed history of early Maryland aimed at younger readers.

Levert, Suzanne. *Edgar Allan Poe.* New York: Chelsea House, 1992. An in-depth biography of the famed writer, poet, and critic.

St. George, Judith. *Mason and Dixon's Line of Fire.* New York: G. P. Putnam's Sons, 1991. A detailed history of the establishment of Maryland's physical boundaries.

Wanning, Esther. *Maryland: The Spirit of America.* New York: Harry N. Abrams, 1998. A brief but informative overview of Maryland's history, culture, and tourist attractions.

Web Sites

▶ Official state web site
www.state.md.us

▶ State capital web site
www.ci.annapolis.md.us

▶ The Maryland State Archives
www.mdarchives.state.md.us

▶ Maryland tourism site
www.mdisfun.org

Recordings

Blake, Eubie. *Memories of You.* Somerville, MA: Biograph, 1993. A collection of some of Eubie Blake's finest jazz and ragtime-era compositions and performances.

Holiday, Billie. *Lady Day: The Complete Billie Holiday on Columbia (1933-1944).* New York: Columbia, 2001. One of the most comprehensive collections of the legendary jazz singer's work released to date.

Note: Page numbers in *italics* refer to maps, illustrations, or photographs.

A

Aberdeen Proving Ground, *14*
Act of Religious Toleration, 30
Adams, John Quincy, 33
Adler, Larry, 33
African Americans, 16, 17, 18, 31, 34, 35
age of population, 18–19
agriculture, 16, *17, 20,* 21–22, 24, 26
airports, 24, 27
Algonquin Indians, 8
Allegheny Mountains, 22
American Visionary Art Museum, 33
animals, 6, 22–23
Annapolis, Maryland, 4, 6
Antietam National Battlefield, 4–5, 36, 44
Appalachian Plateau, 22
Appalachian Ridge and Valley, 21
architecture, 33–34
area, 6
Articles of Confederation, 11
arts, 13, 32–35, 44–45
Artscape, 44
Assateague Indians, 8
Assateague Island National Seashore, 44
attractions, 7, 44–45
Autumn Glory Festival, 44
Avilés, Pedro Menéndez de, 8

B

Babe Ruth Birthplace and Museum, 36
Backbone Mountain, 20, 22
Baltimore, Maryland, 4, 6, 12, 15–19, *18,* 31
Baltimore and Ohio (B&O) Railroad, 12–13, 14, 24
Baltimore Colts, 37
Baltimore Harbor, *9*
Baltimore Harbor Tunnel, 24
Baltimore Museum of Art, 33
Baltimore Opera Company, 32
Baltimore Orioles, 36, 37
Baltimore Ravens, 36, 37
Baltimore Symphony Orchestra, 32
Baltimore/Washington International Airport, 15, 24, 27
Banneker-Douglass Museum, *34*
Barth, John, 35
Barton, Clara, 36–37
baseball, 36, 37

Battle Monument, 34
Battle of Antietam, 13
Battle of Bladensburg, 12
Battle of Monocacy, 13
bird (state symbol), 6
Blake, James Hubert "Eubie," 33
Blue Ridge region, 21
boats and boating, 6, *23*
Boston Port Act, 11
Braxton, Toni, 33
Browning, Meshach, 20
Brunn, Gustav, 27

C

Calvert, Cecilius, 9, 10, 28, 30
Calvert, Charles, 10
Calvert, George, 8–9
Calvert, Leonard, 9–10, 28
Calvert Cliffs State Park, 36
Camden Yards, *37*
Camp David, 4, 14
capitals, 4, 6
capitol building, *29*
Carroll, Charles, 11, *11*
cat (state), 6
Catholics, 9–10
Charles I, 8
Chesapeake and Delaware Canal, 21
Chesapeake and Ohio Canal, 24
Chesapeake Bay, 7, 8, 12, 20–21, 23, *23,* 27, 35
Chesapeake Bay Bridge, *24*
Chesapeake Bay Maritime Museum, 7
Choptank Indians, 8
cities, *5,* 6
Civil War, 13, 24, 28
Claiborne, William, 8, 10
Clancy, Tom, 35
Clara Barton National Historic Site, 36
climate, 21, 22
Coastal Plain, 21
coastline, 20–21
Columbia, Maryland, 6
commerce. *See* economy and commerce
Commissioning Week (U.S. Naval Academy), 44
constitutions, 11, 28–29
Continental Congresses, 11
Coode, John, 10
courts, 30–31
crab races, 7, 45
crown stones, 10
crustacean (state), 6
Crystal Grottoes Cavern, *21*
culture, 13, 32–37
Cumberland Theater, 32

D

Dans Mountain State Park, 36
Deal Island Skipjack Races, 44
Declaration of Independence, 11
Deep Creek Lake, 23
Defenders Day Celebration, 44
Delmarva Peninsula, 20
desegregation, 19
Dixon, Jeremiah, 10
dog (state), 6
Douglass, Frederick, 35, 39, *39*
Dundalk, Maryland, 6

E

Early, Jubal A., 13
Eastern Shore, 20, 31
economy and commerce
    agriculture, 16, *17, 20,* 21–22, 24, 26
    energy, 25
    fishing, 27
    gross state product, 25
    income tax, 15
    industry, 12–13, 16–17
    lottery, 15
    manufacturing, 14, 15, 26
    minerals, 26
    service sector, 26–27
    shipbuilding, 14, 24
    tourism, 7, 15, 27, 35–36
    transportation, 15, 24–25, 27
Eddis, William, 16
education, 18, 19
Eighteenth Amendment, 14
Eisenhower, Dwight D., 14
electricity, 25
employers, 24
energy, 25
Enoch Pratt Free Library, 14
environmental issues, 15, 27
ethnic makeup of Maryland, *17*
events, 44–45
executive branch, 29

F

famous persons, 38–41
farmland, *20,* 21
festivals, 44–45
First Continental Congress, 11
fish (state), 6
fishing industry, 27
Flag Day Ceremonies, 45
flowers, 6, *21,* 23
football, 36
Fort McHenry, 12, *12,* 13, 45
Fussell, Jacob, 7

G

Garrett County, 35

General Assembly, 29, 30
geography of Maryland, 20–23, *22*
Glen Echo, 36
Glendening, Parris N., 24
Goddard Space Flight Center, 4, 7, 24
Godefroy, Maximilian, 34
Governor's Cup Crab Race, 7
Greenbelt, 14-15, 24
gross state product, *25*

H

Hagerstown Valley, 21
Hammet, Dashiell, 35
Hampton Park National Historic Site, 37
Hanson, John, 11
highways, *5*
history of Maryland, 8–13, 42–43
Holiday, Billie, *32,* 33, 41
home rule, 31
Hopkins, Johns, 13–14, 38
horse racing, *36,* 37
House of Delegates, 29, 30

I

immigration, 16–18
income tax, 15
industry, 12–13, 16–17
Inner Harbor Area, 7, *15,* 15, 32
insect (state), 6

J

Janes Island State Park, 35
Johns Hopkins University, 14, 19
Johnson, Thomas, 11
Joseph Meyerhoff Symphony Hall, 32
judicial branch, 30–31

K

Kent Island, 8, 10
Key, Francis Scott, 4, 12, 33
King, Martin Luther, Jr., 15
King and Queen Seat, 36
King William's School, 19
Kuhn, Justus Englehardt, 33–34

L

Lacrosse Hall of Fame & Museum, 36
lakes, 21, 23
Lee, Robert E., 13
legislative branch, 29–30
Liberty Reservoir, 23
lifestyle, 32–37
literature, 34–35, 38–39
local government, 31

Loch Raven Reservoir, 23
lottery, 15
Lyric Opera House, 32

M
manufacturing, 14, 15, 26
maps of Maryland, *5, 22, 25*
Marshall, Thurgood, 33, 41
Maryland Hall for the
 Creative Arts, 32
Maryland Historical Society,
 33
Maryland State Archives
 Museum, 33
Maryland State Fair, 45
Mason, Charles, 10
Mason-Dixon Line, 4, 10, 13
Mattowoman Indians, 8
Mencken, H. L., 35, 40
Merchant's Exchange
 Building, 34
Mikulski, Barbara, 31
Mills, Robert, 34
minerals, 26
Mitchell, Parren, 31
Moore, Lenny, 37
Mothers of Invention, 35
motto (state symbol), 6
museums, 7, 33, *34*
music, 32–33, 35, 41

N
Nanticoke Indians, 8
Nanticoke River, 21
NASA/Goddard Space Flight
 Center, 4, 7, 24
Nash, Ogden, 35
national government, 31. *See
 also* Washington, D.C.
National Hard Crab Derby,
 7, 45
Native Americans, 8–9, 36
natural resources, 26
nickname of Maryland, 4, 14

O
Ocean City, Maryland, 27
Oriole Park, *37*
outdoor activities, 35–36

P
parks, 35–36, 44
Patapsco River, 12
patronage system, 28
Patuxent Indians, 8
Patuxent River, 12

Peabody, George, 13
Peabody Conservatory of
 Music, 14, 19, 32
Peale, Charles Wilson, 34
Peggy Stewart (ship), 11
Piedmont region, 21
Pimlico Race Track, *36*, 37, 45
Piscataway Indians, 8
plant life, 20, 21, *21*, 22–23
Pocomoke Indians, 8
Poe, Edgar Allan, 34–35, *35,
 38*–39
politics and political figures
 Adams, John Quincy, 33
 Articles of Confederation,
  11
 Calvert, Cecilius, 9, 10,
  28, 30
 Calvert, Charles, 10
 Calvert, George, 8–9
 Calvert, Leonard, 9–10, 28
 Carroll, Charles, 11
 Claiborne, William, 10
 Continental Congresses,
  11
 Douglass, Frederick,
  35, *39*
 Eisenhower, Dwight D., 14
 Glendening, Parris N., 24
 governmental structure,
  28–31
 Hanson, John, 11
 international politics, 4
 Johnson, Thomas, 11
 Marshall, Thurgood, 33, 40
 Mikulski, Barbara, 31
 Mitchell, Parren, 31
 national government, 31
 Tubman, Harriet, *39*, 39–40
 Verrazano, Giovanni da, 8
 Washington, George, 4, 34
population, 6, 15, 16–19
Port Covington Yards, *42–43*
Portobago Indians, 8
Potomac River, 9, 15, 21
Potopaco Indians, 8
Pratt, Enoch, 14
Preakness, *36*, 37
Preakness Celebration, 45
Prettyboy Reservoir, 23
Prohibition, 14
Puritans, 9

R
racial makeup of
 Maryland, *17*

railroads, 12–13, 24, *42–43*
rainfall, 21, 22
recreation, 35–36, 44–45
religion, 9–10, 19, 30
reservoirs, 23
Revolutionary War, 4, 10–11,
 24, 28
Ripken, Cal, Jr., 4, 37, 41
rivers, *5,* 12, 15, 21
Robinson, Frank, 37
Rocks State Park, 36
Ross, Robert, 12
Ruth, George Herman "Babe,"
 36, 37, *40,* 40-41

S
St. Clement's Island, 9
St. John's College, 19
St. Michaels, Maryland, 7
seal of Maryland, *28*
seaports, 27
Second Continental
 Congress, 11
segregation, 19
Senate, 30
service sector, 26–27
settlers, 9, 16
shipbuilding, 14, 24
shipping, 12–13
Silver Spring, Maryland, 6
Sinclair, Upton, 4
slavery, 4, 13, 28
Smith, John, 8
snowfall, 21, 22
song (state), 6
Space Flight Center, 4, 7, 24
sports, 36, 37, 40, 41
"The Star-Spangled Banner"
 (Key), 4, 12, 33
State House, 7, 29
statehood, 6, 11
Strawberry Festival, 45
Susquehannock Indians, 8,
 36
Susquehanna River, 21

T
Takoma Park Folk Festival, 45
Taocomaco Indians, 8
temperature, 21, 22
time line of Maryland history,
 42–43
tobacco, 24
tourism, 7, 15, 27, 35–36
Towsontown Spring
 Festival, 45

transportation, 15, 24–25, 27
tree (state), 6
Tubman, Harriet, 4, *39,* 39–40
Tyler, Anne, 35

U
Unitas, Johnny, 37
U.S. Naval Academy, 4, *19,* 44
U.S. Naval Academy
 Museum, 33
University of Maryland, 19

V
Verrazano, Giovanni da, 8

W
War of 1812, 4, 11–12
Warren, Edward, 7
Washington, D.C., 4, 15, 26–27
Washington, George, 4, 34
Washington Monument,
 33, *33*
Waterfowl Festival, 45
waterways, *5*
Webb, Chick, 33
Weems, Mason Locke, 34
Weinberg Center for
 the Arts, 32
Western Shore, 20, 31
White, Andrew, 34
Wicomico Indians, 8
wildlife, 6, 20–23
World War I, 14, 24
World War II, 15, 24

Y
Yaocomaco Indians, 8, 9
Youghiogheny River, 21

Z
Zappa, Frank Vincent, 35